METHADONE

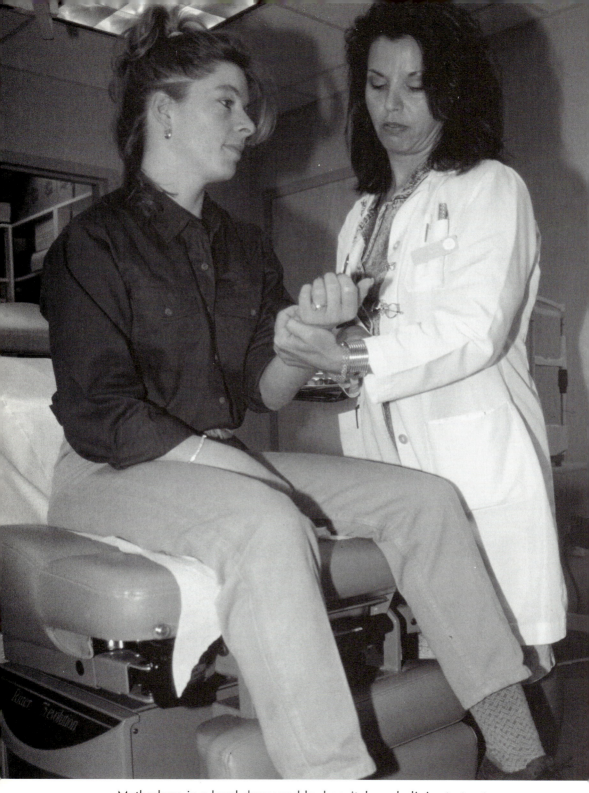

Methadone is a legal drug used by hospitals and clinics to treat patients addicted to heroin.

METHADONE

Carolyn Simpson

THE ROSEN PUBLISHING GROUP, INC.
NEW YORK

The people pictured in this book are only models; they in no way practice or endorse the activities illustrated. Captions serve only to explain the subjects of the photographs and do not imply a connection between the real-life models and the staged situations shown. News agency photographs are exceptions.

Published in 1997 by The Rosen Publishing Group, Inc.
29 East 21st Street, New York, NY 10010

First Edition

Library of Congress Cataloging-in-Publication Data
Simpson, Carolyn.
    Methadone / Carolyn Simpson.
        p. cm. — (The drug abuse prevention library)
    Includes bibliographical references and index.
    Summary: Explains what methadone is, what it does, the pros and cons of its use as a treatment for heroin addiction, and possible abuses of this drug.
    ISBN 0-8239-2286-3
    1. Methadone maintenance—Juvenile literature.
2. Heroin habit—Treatment—Juvenile literature.
[1. Methadone maintenance.   2. Heroin.
3. Drugs.]   I. Title.   II. Series.
RC568.M4S55   1997
616.86′32061—dc21   96-54270
                                                          CIP
                                                          AC

Manufactured in the United States of America

Contents

Introduction

Many people assume that methadone treatment is the best way to treat heroin addiction. After all, they reason, any substance that can help an addict quit using heroin and rebuild a normal life must be a miracle.

Some methadone supporters say that while methadone is addictive itself, it's okay because users replace a harmful drug, heroin, with a less harmful drug, methadone.

But is methadone really the answer? Users of methadone, and the scientists who study it, have discovered that methadone creates its own problems.

This book will explore the pros and cons of methadone use. The first chapter discusses why people were originally so enthusiastic about methadone treatment. We will also examine the dangers of heroin addiction and the search to find ways to help heroin addicts stop using it. Withdrawal from heroin is difficult and time consuming; most addicts return to heroin when they can't handle the withdrawal symptoms. Methadone eliminates the craving for heroin that addicts experience.

The second chapter discusses what goes on in hospitals and clinics that use methadone to treat heroin addicts. It explores the benefits of methadone treatment. Consider the following:

1) Only 50 percent of heroin users who quit with the help of methadone have a relapse (return to using heroin) after treatment, compared to the 75–80 percent of heroin users trying to kick the heroin habit without methadone.
2) Methadone allows heroin addicts to function in society without always wondering when and where they will get more of the drug—their next fix. They can become productive members of the community despite being addicted to heroin.

8

3) Methadone is given orally, not by injection. This eliminates the problems that arise from users who inject heroin directly into their veins. Heroin addicts may suffer collapsed veins and, worse, sometimes use dirty needles that can spread HIV (human immunodeficiency virus), the virus that causes AIDS (acquired immunodeficiency syndrome).

4) According to The Lindesmith Center, a drug policy research institute, it costs an average of $4,000 a year to maintain a patient on methadone while keeping a user in jail costs $20,000 to $40,000 per year.

There is, however, another side to methadone treatment. Chapters 3 and 4 describe the drawbacks of methadone. Some of the arguments against it include:

1) Methadone is deceptive because some see it as a "treatment" for heroin addiction, but it is just as addictive as heroin. Technically, users are substituting one addictive drug for another.

2) People using methadone are not necessarily learning to cope with

the problems that led them to use
heroin initially; after all, they are
continuing to use drugs.

3) Many methadone users need to live
near clinics so they can continue to
get their daily doses of methadone.
This can be inconvenient and may
discourage those who need treatment from sticking with a program.

4) A methadone clinic can be an
unwanted addition to a neighborhood. Clinics are often blamed for
bringing an unpleasant element into
some communities.

5) Methadone use presents a problem
for pregnant women. Heroin disrupts a woman's menstrual cycle,
making it difficult for her to con-
ceive. Methadone, however, allows a
female addict's body to return to
normal, so she is able to become
pregnant; but once she is pregnant,
she is still dependent on methadone, which can be dangerous to a
developing fetus (unborn baby).

Methadone treatment is a complicated
issue. This book will help you to look at
the issues surrounding methadone and its
use as a treatment for heroin addiction.

When heroin addicts crash, they suffer from intense withdrawal symptoms, such as runny noses, watery eyes, and excessive sweating.

CHAPTER 1

What Is Methadone?

*S*harla knocked on her friend's door. Katie hadn't been to school in days. Sharla banged on the door louder and then called out to Katie.

"Go away. I'm busy," Katie responded.

Sharla tried to look in the window. "Let me in; I'm worried about you," she said.

Katie appeared to be going through all the cupboards in the kitchen. Pots and pans were scattered across the floor. Drawers were turned upside down.

"What's going on in there?" Sharla asked.

Finally the door opened. Katie looked as if she had a bad case of the flu. Her nose was

12 | *runny, her eyes were watery, and sweat rolled down her face.*

"I need to borrow some money," she said.

"What for?" Sharla asked. "You look sick; you ought to be in bed."

"I'll be okay; I just need to get something."

"In the kitchen? Looks like you've torn this place apart," Sharla said, looking around. She looked more closely at Katie. "You told me you stopped doing heroin."

"I'm going to stop," Katie replied.

"I don't think you can. Look at you."

Katie started tearing apart another cupboard. "Help me find my mom's old silverware. I think there are a few more pieces left."

Sharla cringed. "You've been selling her silver?"

"Mom doesn't use it. She's just saving it for me, and I need it right now."

"Katie, you need help, not more drugs."

Katie turned around suddenly. "I need one more fix," she pleaded. "One more, and I swear I'll quit."

"How could you do this to yourself?" Sharla cried, sickened by her friend's behavior.

Katie sank down on the floor. "I never meant to do it. I was just going to smoke some pot, but everyone else was shooting up. I was just going to try it. I thought I wouldn't get hooked if I only did it once in a while."

"You've got to get help," Sharla said.

"Don't you think I've tried?" Katie snapped. "It's not that easy. If I go a little time without the stuff I feel awful, and all I can think about is getting one more fix. I must have pawned most of Mom's good silver."

"You need to go to a treatment center," Sharla said.

"Are you kidding?" Katie said. "They would just watch me suffer."

"You could get methadone," Sharla said. "People take it to get off heroin. Let's call a drug abuse hot line. They can help us out. Come on, there's a number listed in the front of every phone book."

The History of Methadone

Methadone is a legal drug used to treat people addicted to heroin. It can only be obtained with a doctor's prescription.

Methadone was discovered in Germany, but was not used as a treatment method for heroin addiction until the mid 1960s. The experiments of Drs. Vincent Dole and Marie Nyswander

Methadone allows heroin addicts to function normally and carry on daily chores, such as doing homework, without suffering from withdrawal symptoms.

showed that methadone blocked the
craving for heroin. While the user did not
get high, the methadone kept the heroin
addict from suffering the effects of withdrawal. This drug appeared to be a miracle cure for heroin addiction. Its only
drawback was that it was addictive as
well.

You may wonder why anyone would
want to replace one addiction with
another. The answer is complex. Let's
begin with understanding why heroin
addiction is such a problem in society.

A History of Narcotics

Heroin is a narcotic analgesic. Narcotic
drugs put users in a daze and cloud their
thinking. Analgesics are pain relievers.
Narcotic analgesics are drugs that put
people in a dreamy state where they feel
no pain. Users lose much of their aware-
ness of things around them. Narcotic
analgesics are a class of pain-relieving
drugs called opiates.

Opiates are made from the milky juice
of the poppy plant. When this juice dries,
it hardens into a brown substance called
opium. Opium has a long history. For
more than 5,000 years, people have used
it as medicine. It has been used to treat

16 | both pain and diarrhea (since opium has a constipating effect).

Opium is grown in many Asian countries. Heroin, also made from the poppy plant, is easily smuggled into North America because it is relatively odorless. However, it is against the law to transport it, possess it, use it, or sell it.

People turned to opium and drugs made from opium for pain relief before the discovery of aspirin in 1898. They didn't realize that they would become addicted until it was too late. Morphine, a potent form of opium, was sold in cough suppressant medicines and in teething gels. It could be found in products on grocery store shelves as late as 1900. The invention of the hypodermic needle in 1853 allowed addicts to

The invention of the hypodermic needle allowed drug users to inject the drugs directly into their veins, increasing the drugs' effects. As a result, users became addicted more easily.

inject morphine directly into their veins, greatly increasing the drug's effects.

Morphine as Medicine

The American Civil War (1861–1865) increased the large-scale medical use of morphine as a pain reliever. Because conditions were so unsanitary in army camps, soldiers often became sick with dysentery (a particularly bad case of diarrhea). Many died. Morphine offered pain relief and a temporary cure for diarrhea. Doctors could do little else to relieve the suffering of sick and wounded soldiers besides giving out morphine. This was before they realized morphine was addictive. By the war's end, so many soldiers were addicted to morphine that people called morphine addiction "the soldier's disease."

Heroin Comes on the Scene

After scientists realized the dangers of morphine addiction, they tried to develop a drug to cure the addiction. Heroin was discovered in 1897 and thought to be that miracle cure. Unfortunately, heroin proved to be three times more addictive than morphine. Not only did people develop a tolerance to heroin (requiring

18 increasingly more of the drug to feel the same relief), they also developed a tolerance to the other opiates, such as opium and morphine.

By 1924, the manufacture of heroin was banned in the United States. However, people still manufactured and sold it illegally. Addicts would pay any price to maintain their habits, and dealers were eager to make a profit.

Who Abused Heroin?

In the 1940s, musicians began dabbling with heroin because they thought it would help them handle the strain of playing long performances and staying up late in the recording studio. Billie Holiday was a famous blues singer whose career was ruined by heroin addiction. In the 1960s, a time of heavy drug experimentation, heroin use became more widespread. Wealthy professionals soon began experimenting with heroin. Many who experimented with other stimulating drugs used heroin to slow them down afterward. Unfortunately, they ended up with a double addiction.

Recently, heroin use has become popular again. Back in the 1980s heroin was not used by many people because

Actor River Phoenix died at the age of twenty-three from an overdose of heroin and cocaine.

20 of its high price, low-level purity, and because many were afraid of contracting HIV through dirty needles. Heroin is now making a comeback because it is cheaper and purer. The purity enables users to snort or smoke the drug rather than inject it.

The young deaths of singer Kurt Cobain of the band Nirvana and actor River Phoenix have been linked to heroin. More recently, actor Robert Downey, Jr. was arrested for cocaine and heroin possession.

Dangers of Heroin

There are several dangers associated with heroin and intravenous (IV) drug use. Aside from dulling the senses, heroin ruins the body's ability to produce its own natural painkillers, called endorphins. Endorphins reduce pain intensity as well as control the appetite, the feeling of well-being, and the release of sex hormones. When a person injects heroin, the body stops producing endorphins. Heroin imitates endorphins, fooling the body and causing it to stop producing its own endorphins. Once a person starts taking heroin, his or her primary pain relief is through the drug. Even when an addict stops taking heroin, the body doesn't immediately start producing endorphins again. During withdrawal from heroin, the addict feels extremely sick and experiences sweating, a runny nose, watery eyes, uneven sleep, vomiting, diarrhea, and abdominal cramps. Most people can't tolerate the sick feeling and experience tremendous cravings for heroin, which has replaced the body's endorphins. It is extremely difficult to stay off heroin.

Developing Tolerance

As addicts continue to use heroin, they need to increase their doses because they develop tolerance for the drug. Heroin acts as a depressant on the central nervous system. If taken with other drugs that act in the same way, the combination can make the person stop breathing, and he or she can die.

Even before addiction occurs, heroin affects the user's ability to concentrate and to think and speak clearly. It also destroys the user's appetite.

Dangers of Injecting

Injecting, or "shooting," heroin causes other health problems. Heroin destroys a user's health by weakening the immune

22 system, reducing his or her ability to fight off infection. Injecting into overused veins can cause them to collapse which can restrict the flow of blood. Needles that have been used by more than one person can carry life-threatening infections, including hepatitis (inflammation of the liver) and endocarditis (inflammation of the heart lining). Worse, dirty needles can carry HIV, the virus that causes AIDS, for which there is no cure.

Although some users believe heroin is not dangerous if it is smoked or snorted, the consequences can be deadly if they overdose. Overdoses can happen if addicts inject heroin that is purer than they are used to. Since heroin is illegal, its purity and quality are unregulated by government agencies.

Most dealers "cut" their own heroin. Cutting means adding other "ingredients" to increase the amount of the drug that they can sell. When a drug has been cut, the buyer has no idea how pure the drug actually is or what other ingredients have been added to it. If an addict usually uses a certain amount of heroin that is 5 percent pure and then takes the same amount of heroin that happens to be 50 percent pure, he or she will overdose.

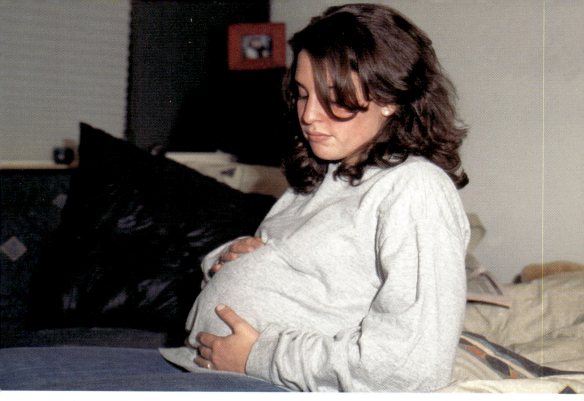

Women who use heroin during their pregnancy can seriously injure or even kill their unborn baby.

Heroin can disrupt a woman's menstrual cycle, making it very difficult for her to become pregnant. However, if a woman does somehow become pregnant, heroin can be fatal for the unborn baby. Heroin increases the chance that the baby will be born prematurely, stillborn, or with birth defects. Just as the mother is addicted to heroin, so is the baby. Upon birth, the baby faces the painful task of withdrawal. A heroin-addicted baby is easily upset, cries more often, and has other problems that will show up as the child develops.

Maintaining a heroin habit can be very costly. Addicts often resort to stealing from family members and friends to support their habits.

The Impact of Heroin Addiction on Society

Drug addiction not only affects users; it also affects their families, friends, and communities. Maintaining a heroin habit can be costly (an average of $100 a day), so an addict is constantly thinking of ways to get money. Often that money is stolen from family members and local businesses. At the same time, heroin destroys the addict's ability to think clearly, to concentrate on tasks, and to handle everyday responsibilities. Addicts are unable to hold down regular jobs for long periods of time.

Families can't function when relying on a user who is unable to hold down a job or stay out of jail. Statistics indicate that most addicts start using heroin before the age of twenty-five. Under heroin's influence, young people stop caring about school-work or career goals. To support their habits, they often become involved in crime, usually burglary or prostitution. Teens will even sell off their family posses-sions to get money for drugs.

We have discussed the many problems caused by heroin. Heroin addicts do not only hurt themselves, but they hurt the rest of society as well. Heroin addicts are often out of control. Their actions are controlled by their addiction. They need help in regaining control of their lives. For these reasons, many people see meth-adone as the solution to the terrible problem of heroin addiction in society.

CHAPTER 2

The Benefits of Methadone Treatment

John took a seat in the dayroom. As soon as the other patients received their medication, Samir, the medication aide, called out to him.

"Are you ready to go?"

John nodded. He was starting to feel sick; his stomach ached.

Samir unlocked the door to their unit, and the two of them walked through the hallway to the locked area where the drugs were kept. It was on the other side of the building.

Reggie, the nurse, had set up cups of orange juice. She handed a cup to John and watched as he drank it.

John crumpled the cup and handed it back.

"You know the routine, John," Reggie said. "Open your mouth."

"Oh, come on," John said. "How could anyone fake swallowing this stuff?" He opened his mouth and moved his tongue around.

"It's been done," Reggie said, as she checked his mouth.

"What's my dose, Reggie?" John asked.

"It's where it should be," she answered, jotting something down in her chart.

"How come you never tell me what it is?" he complained.

"It's policy; you know that," Reggie said.

"Well, I think I should be getting a bigger dose. I start feeling sick before I get it these days. It's not holding me anymore."

Samir looked annoyed. "John," he said, "you don't need to know your dose. You're always thinking it's time to increase it. Methadone isn't like heroin. You don't have to keep increasing it. There's a range where you'll function just fine, and you're there."

John shrugged. "I just don't want you guys to start decreasing my dosage too soon."

Reggie smiled sympathetically. "John, we're not going to rush you because we don't

28 *want you going back to heroin. The methadone will keep you from going through withdrawal, but you still have to work with the therapists to fix the rest of your life so you don't fall back into the same trap."*

John nodded. "I know; I just wish the whole process took less time."

The Benefits of Methadone

Because heroin addiction has such a negative impact on society due to the crimes committed to support a habit and the loss of productive citizens, an addiction to methadone is seen by some as the lesser of two evils. Addicts can still function normally on methadone. They can hold down a job or attend school; they don't have to worry about how they are going to get their next fix, and they won't have that craving for heroin.

About 80 percent of the people who try to quit heroin eventually relapse. It is extremely difficult to quit heroin. Methadone offers a safe alternative, despite its addictive nature. It offers the heroin addict a way out. Being on methadone gives the user a chance to get control of his or her life before it's too late. Going "cold turkey" (trying to quit

on willpower alone) rarely works with
heroin. Even if the addict makes it past
withdrawal, he or she still faces up to ten
years of daily heroin cravings. The cravings don't end as soon as withdrawal
does. Even if a person eventually has to
withdraw from methadone, the symptoms
of withdrawal are supposedly less painful
than withdrawal from heroin.

Standard Methadone Treatment

Usually, heroin addicts are hospitalized
when they want methadone treatment.
They participate in a program that often
includes both methadone and therapy.
Once they successfully complete the
program, they are allowed to leave. Then
they can continue to receive methadone
as an outpatient (someone who goes to
the hospital or clinic for treatment, then
leaves without having to stay overnight).
Methadone is a synthetic form of the
opiates, but is equally addictive. Therefore, it can only be given under the
careful supervision of doctors and nurses.

According to federal guidelines, a
patient must be eighteen years old to re-
quest methadone treatment. He or she
must also have at least a one-year heroin
addiction and a physical dependence on

30 the drug. Physical dependence means a person has developed a tolerance to the drug and will experience withdrawal symptoms without the substance. In order to avoid withdrawal, the person has to keep increasing the dose or take the same amount more frequently.

A person between the ages of sixteen and eighteen can enter methadone treatment with parental consent, if he or she is emancipated (officially declared an adult by the courts), or if he or she has had two prior attempts at detoxification or non-methadone maintenance treatment.

What happens once the patient has been admitted to a methadone maintenance program? He or she receives methadone to help avoid the withdrawal that comes from giving up heroin. Methadone comes in liquid, powder, and tablet form. The liquid or powder dose is mixed in orange juice or Tang, and the patient drinks it. Otherwise, the patient takes the dose in pill form. Under either circumstance, the patient will have to swallow the methadone in front of a nurse. At the beginning of treatment, the patient is watched carefully to make sure that he or she has swallowed all the methadone. This is to ensure that patients

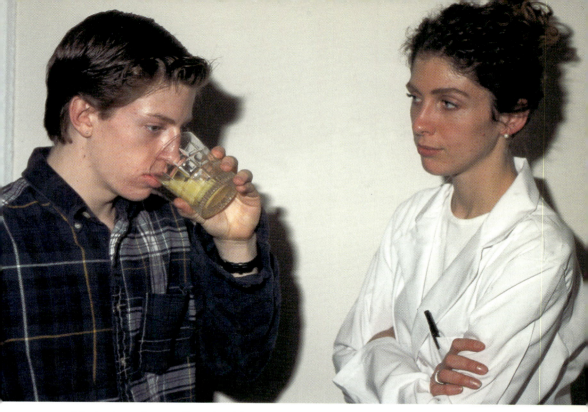

Methadone is usually mixed in orange juice or Tang. A nurse usually dispenses the methadone and watches the patient carefully to insure that he or she swallows all the methadone.

don't spit out or pretend to take the methadone only to sell it on the streets later.

Random Drug Screens
Methadone patients are randomly asked to give urine samples to determine how much of the drug is in their systems. If they're continuing to abuse other substances, that shows up in the tests, too. If their methadone level isn't as high as their oral dose indicates it should be, the staff knows that the patient is probably not swallowing all of the medicine.

32 | *The Difference Between Heroin and Methadone*

A person taking heroin feels an initial rush and then warmth spreading throughout the body. The heroin then puts him or her in a stupor, and he or she is likely to lay around, feeling good and letting his or her mind drift. Clearly, someone on heroin is not in the frame of mind to concentrate on anything.

With methadone, addicts do not feel the high that comes from heroin. Nor will they experience difficulty concentrating. They simply lose the craving for heroin and the painful symptoms of withdrawal that might make them turn to heroin again.

Taking Methadone

Taking methadone orally eliminates the problems associated with IV use. People taking methadone don't face the risk of collapsed veins and contracting HIV from dirty needles. An oral dose has a slower onset (in other words, users won't feel the effects as quickly), but the effects last longer. Unlike heroin, methadone's effects last from twenty-four to thirty-six hours. The person being treated with methadone will still be able to function

At the beginning, a person usually needs to be hospitalized to receive methadone treatment.

The most successful methadone treatment programs combine counseling with the methadone treatment.

to face the same problems that may have caused them to abuse drugs. Family therapy may help resolve those problems by enabling family members to see how their behavior might have contributed to the problem.

Patients may or may not have therapy sessions that go along with the methadone treatment. Ideally, therapy should take place several times a day: group therapy once a day, individual or family therapy sessions twice a week, and occupational therapy and support groups, such as Narcotics Anonymous (NA), in the evening.

Methadone and Other Drugs

Methadone addicts won't make a lasting recovery unless they change their lifestyles. That's why the most successful methadone clinics combine counseling with drug treatment. Drug addicts must learn to recognize the temptations of any drug and how to avoid them.

Recovering heroin addicts should stay away from alcohol because it can affect their judgment. A recovering addict who continues to drink is not thinking clearly. Under the influence, he or she might

Recovering heroin addicts should avoid alcohol. Alcohol can cloud a person's judgment. Under alcohol's influence, a recovering heroin addict may believe it is okay to use heroin again.

think it's okay to try heroin just one more time.

Alcohol also damages the liver, and the liver is important in metabolizing methadone. When a person takes methadone, some of it is stored in the liver to be released later into the system. This is why a person only needs regular doses about every twenty-four hours. If the liver isn't working properly, the person won't be able to store the methadone. He or she will have trouble handling dosages given on a twenty-four-hour schedule.

Some people mistakenly think methadone can treat all drug problems. It only treats those addicted to heroin. Methadone has no effect on cocaine, alcohol, or marijuana addictions.

How Long Do Outpatients Stay on Methadone?

Taking methadone can be a permanent thing, or outpatients can try to come off methadone at some point when they think they can handle withdrawal. Taking it permanently doesn't mean they will have to stay in a hospital for the rest of their lives. Outpatients usually visit local clinics for their methadone

40 doses. Statistics are not yet available on the number of people who stay off heroin through methadone maintenance treatment. There are approximately 100,000 patients in methadone treatment in the United States, but not all patients will choose to continue methadone maintenance treatment all of their lives. Some things we do know: 50 percent of those who quit taking methadone under the best of circumstances will relapse within three years. This is better than the 80 percent who relapse when they quit heroin without methadone.

The people who stand the best chance of remaining off heroin when they have completed methadone treatment are older people who have stable jobs and incomes, a satisfactory marriage, and a supportive family. Those people who are more likely to relapse easily are younger addicts from unstable situations. These people often lack supportive families and friends and jobs, or they are involved in a criminal lifestyle.

Many people believe methadone maintenance treatment is perfectly safe for lifetime use. Others are worried about how such long-term treatment will affect young adults. Nonetheless, most people

agree that at present methadone offers
the best chance for heroin users to
overcome their addiction and regain
control of their lives.

Methadone treatment can be inconvenient. Outpatients need to live close to a clinic because they need to go to the clinic daily for their methadone dosage.

CHAPTER 3

The Drawbacks of Methadone Treatment

*A*s mentioned in the introduction, methadone treatment comes with its own set of problems. For one thing, methadone is an addictive drug itself. While it's effective in breaking an addiction to heroin, users are still dependent on a drug. Users relying on a drug, even a legal one, do not necessarily learn to change behavior patterns or solve problems. Some people mistakenly believe methadone is the answer to all their problems. Methadone becomes another cycle of addiction if the user doesn't learn to change his or her lifestyle.

Methadone treatment can also be inconvenient. Even though users need only

44 | one dose each day, they still can't be far from the methadone clinic.

A new, longer-lasting drug by the name of Orlaam, or LAAM, has been approved by the Food and Drug Administration as an alternative to methadone. Unlike methadone, which must be taken daily, this new drug is only taken three times per week. While methadone users who show progress and test negative for other drugs for two years are allowed to take home doses, patients on LAAM will not be able to do that. This is because of the strength of the drug and the potential for illegal sales on the street. But whether patients take methadone or LAAM, they will still need to plan their lives around their visits to a clinic.

Not Everyone Wants to Quit Heroin

Some people who enter methadone treatment have no intention of getting off drugs. These people go into treatment because they can't afford heroin, or it has suddenly become dangerous on the streets for them. Entering methadone clinics for treatment keeps them supplied so that they don't suffer withdrawal. They soon return to the streets and resume their heroin habit.

Terence was a psychiatric aide at an inner-city methadone clinic. He liked to sit around with the patients and talk about their situations when they weren't busy with therapy. That way he had a better idea of how each patient was doing.

Charlotte never seemed to participate in therapy, although she always attended the meetings. She seemed to look at the other patients with disgust and usually walked out of the room when Terence came in.

The other aides thought Charlotte was just having a hard time kicking heroin. Terence thought something else was going on. One day, he found her alone in the dayroom.

"I like to be straight with people," he said. "I wonder why you're here. I don't think you really want to give up heroin."

"Oh, yeah?" Charlotte said. "Then why would I put myself through all this?"

"Oh, I can think of some reasons," Terence said. "Maybe your supplier is in jail. Maybe you're supposed to be in jail yourself. Maybe you owe people some money and you're hiding out. Maybe you're out of money. See? There are lots of reasons."

Charlotte looked unimpressed. "Do you say that about all your patients?"

"Only some of them," he answered. "I told you I believed in being honest."

46

"Well, I'm here to mend my ways," Charlotte said.

"So, tell me what it was like for you out on the streets."

"Look, it's rough enough out there. I don't need to deal with more of the same stuff in here," said Charlotte. "Okay, so maybe I'm not interested in therapy. All I want is the methadone so I don't feel bad anymore. Is there anything wrong in that?"

"How about some vocational training? Don't you want to get a new start in life?" Terence asked.

"Oh, don't be a fool. I never even finished seventh grade. I already know how to take care of myself. Sometimes I just run out of money." She glared at Terence.

"I guess you're telling me that you're here until you can go back out on the streets," Terence said.

"Something like that," Charlotte answered. "Look, I need the methadone. Really."

"Okay," Terence said. "But come back sometime when you really want to change."

Contradictory Studies

While methadone has been reported to improve the immune system of former heroin addicts, one study has found some contradictory information. In a study that followed several patients taking 100 milligrams of methadone daily, the patients were found to have lowered pulse and respiration rates. These same patients showed signs of social withdrawal, tiredness, lack of energy and enthusiasm, and a "diminished sense of well-being."

Clearly, not all studies support the idea that methadone treatment is good for people's health.

Dangers to Pregnant Women

Taking heroin is, of course, much more dangerous to the pregnant female than taking methadone. However, there is a problem. Fifty percent of heroin addicts lose interest in sex and therefore don't engage in sex as much. In addition, heroin disrupts women's menstrual cycles, making it less likely that they would be able to become pregnant.

Methadone normalizes the addict's sexual activity and menstrual cycle, so she is able to become pregnant. However, methadone is not recommended for use during pregnancy. If a woman wants to take methadone but is less than three months pregnant, a doctor will probably

Babies born to mothers who took methadone during their pregnancy will often be more restless, cry more often, and likely have emotional problems that worsen as they grow older.

advise against starting the methadone until after the baby is born.

The first three months of a pregnancy are very important because this is the time that the baby develops its organs and limbs. Methadone can be especially dangerous during this period because it can affect the baby's development. Organs and limbs may not develop normally.

If the woman is past three months pregnant (or has been on methadone when she discovers she's pregnant), she

will likely continue methadone treatment. **49**
The risk to the baby is greater from withdrawal at that point. Nonetheless, babies born to mothers taking methadone will be restless, cry more often, and likely show emotional problems that will worsen as they grow older.

Dangers of Overdosing

It is also possible to overdose on methadone. There are two ways to overdose on methadone. If methadone is combined with other drugs, the user can die from the combination. A person can also overdose when he or she has been taking methadone for a period of time and then goes back to using heroin. Some people don't realize that they can't go back to their previous level of usage. If they resume where they left off, they will overdose.

CHAPTER 4

Abuses in Methadone Clinics

*W*hile methadone itself has some drawbacks, so does the administration of methadone in clinics and hospitals.

Methadone Mills

There is money involved in operating a methadone clinic. Public funds are available to cover the operation. Unfortunately, past events have shown us that some clinic operators were more interested in the money than in the service being performed. These clinics, called methadone mills, were more interested in numbers served than in providing social rehabilitation or vocational training.

Without therapy programs, many patients

did not learn to solve the problems that
led them to use drugs.

When original studies showed how promising methadone treatment could be, they were based on misleading data. The original programs were small, and the nursing staffs had no trouble monitoring their patients. The programs are not as promising when applied to larger populations (such as numbers commonly served today), because the staffs cannot supervise all their patients. Thus, methadone treatment is not as effective as the original reports indicated (unless strict supervision is provided).

Criminal Activity

Naturally, there is criminal activity associated with heroin addiction because of the high costs to support an average habit. The addict also can't hold down a job. However, some addicts continue their criminal ways after their switch to methadone. The main source for methadone sold on the streets comes from patients in methadone programs. Some patients get doctors to prescribe more of the drug than their bodies actually need to prevent withdrawal. Then they

52 | use only what they need and sell the rest.

Patients in methadone clinics can spit their dose out into a sponge (to squeeze out later and sell) or they try to split their take-home doses into two parts—one for themselves and the other to sell. According to an article that appeared in the *New York Times*, a dose of methadone can be sold for $25 to $40 on the streets.

It doesn't take long for a clinic staff to catch on to these practices. This is why patients are watched carefully as they take their doses, and why take-home doses are so hard to obtain. Doctors have also learned to maintain their patients on the lowest possible dose to avoid withdrawal symptoms. This makes it difficult for patients to sell even the smallest portion, because it would mean facing withdrawal themselves. Also, the patients are randomly asked to give urine samples. These tests help the staff to determine if patients are abusing other drugs or if their methadone level is where it should be.

You may wonder why anyone would buy methadone on the street. This usually happens when users can't get or afford heroin. It is possible for someone to

Some people believe that methadone clinics bring many problems usually associated with drug use, such as crime and violence, to communities.

become addicted to methadone first. This is called primary methadone addiction. This happens when an individual becomes addicted to methadone before ever trying heroin or the other opiates.

Clinics in Neighborhoods

You might think that communities would welcome methadone clinics because that would mean opportunities for addicts to get off heroin. However, many people are reluctant to have a methadone clinic come into their neighborhood.

54

Some people believe that having methadone clinics in their neighborhoods can attract problems usually associated with drugs, such as crime and violence.

Some methadone users continue abusing other drugs, thinking that methadone is helping them kick the worst of their habits. But as mentioned in an earlier chapter, methadone has no effect on other drug addictions. People who go to methadone clinics that don't offer therapy or vocational services don't learn to deal with the problems that led them to use drugs.

Alternatives to Methadone

Several alternatives to methadone treatment exist. Going cold turkey rarely works. There are, however, programs that concentrate on counseling and social rehabilitation rather than offering drugs. Phoenix House Foundation is one of the largest programs like this in the United States. Individuals may stay in a community atmosphere to learn the skills needed to turn their lives around and stay away from drugs.

Many Narcotics Anonymous peer support groups discourage drug use of any kind.

Conclusion

*I*s methadone the lesser of two evils or does it create more problems for recovering heroin addicts? In deciding this, you have to consider the main issue.

Addiction to heroin is one of the hardest habits to break. If a heroin addict has no support system (no family involvement, no income or friends), that person is unlikely to break his or her habit on willpower alone. The craving for heroin can last up to ten years, whereas withdrawal symptoms may go away after just ten days. If a drug, even an addictive one, can stop the craving for heroin, should it be used?

56 Think about the issues that have been discussed in this book concerning the use of methadone.

1) Methadone helps heroin addicts kick their habits by stopping the craving and withdrawal symptoms of the drug. The downside of this is that it only postpones the withdrawal symptoms one has to experience to be drug free.

2) Methadone allows the individual to be resocialized (hold down a job, support his or her family), but some methadone clinics don't emphasize social rehabilitation.

3) Methadone restores a woman's menstrual cycle, but also restores her libido (interest in sex), which probably will increase her sexual activity. This can lead to the increased chance of pregnancy (which can create a whole new set of problems).

4) Methadone eliminates the need for addicts to turn to criminal activities to support an illegal heroin habit, but methadone can be stolen from clinics and sold illegally on the streets.

5) Methadone is a miracle to some, a
   crutch for others.

For those addicts who are unable to
cope with heroin withdrawal, methadone
may be the only way to keep them from
returning to heroin. And heroin is much
more destructive than methadone. Heroin
destroys a person mentally (making it
harder to concentrate or care about anything or anyone) and physically (making
him or her more susceptible to deadly
diseases, such as AIDS). Heroin destroys
families because addicts neglect everyone
for their costly habits. It destroys communities by destroying families first. If
methadone treatment can cure heroin
addiction, it has accomplished a great
deal.

However, for some people methadone
is a way to continue a cycle of addiction
legally. Methadone can buy time for a
person to work out the problems that led
him or her to drugs. That's not a negative, as long as the person is working to-
ward putting his or her life together and
eventually getting off all drugs.

Glossary—
Explaining New Words

analgesic Pain reliever.

cold turkey Getting off a drug without help from another substance.

dependence When the body has developed tolerance to a drug and will suffer withdrawal symptoms if deprived of that drug.

detoxification Stopping the use of all drugs and eliminating them from the body.

endorphins Properties natural in the body that lower the intensity of pain.

intravenous (IV) Administration (of a drug) through the veins.

narcotic A drug that puts a person in a

dreamy, confused state.

opiates Opium, morphine, and heroin (all made from the poppy plant) that are considered narcotic analgesics and are extremely addictive.

outpatient A patient who visits a hospital or clinic regularly for treatment but doesn't stay overnight.

rehabilitation Restoring a person to good health or good behavior.

stillborn When a baby is dead at birth.

stupor A dazed state with little or no feeling.

synthetic Not found in nature; made by humans through a chemical process.

tolerance Needing to increase drug use in order to maintain the same effect from the drug.

withdrawal The extreme physical and mental distress experienced by users when they give up a drug their bodies have become dependent on.

Where to Go for Help

Hot Lines
National Drug and Alcohol Treatment
   Routing Service
(800) 662-HELP
PRIDE (Drug Information Line)
(800) 241-9746
Youth Crisis Hot Line
(800) 448-4663

Organizations
American Council for Drug Education
204 Monroe Street
Rockville, MD 20852
(301) 294-0600
(800) 488-DRUG

National Abuse Center
5530 Wisconsin Avenue, NW
Washington, DC 20015
(800) 333-2294

National Association of Alcohol and Drug
   Abuse Counselors
3717 Columbia Pike, Suite 300
Arlington, VA 22204

(800) 548-0497

National Clearinghouse for Alcohol and
  Drug Information
P.O. Box 2345
Rockville, MD 20847-2345
(301) 468-2600
Web site: http://www.health.org
e-mail: info@prevline.health.org

National Council on Alcohol and Drug
  Dependence (NCADD)
12 West 21st Street
New York, NY 10010
(212) 206-6770
(800) 622-2255

Phoenix House Drugs Don't Work
  Program
(800) 883-3784

Resource Center on Substance Abuse
  Prevention and Disabilities
1819 L Street, Suite 300
Washington, DC 20036
(202) 628-8080
(800) 628-8442

IN CANADA

Alcohol and Drug Dependency
  Information and Counseling Services
2471 1/2 Portage Avenue, #2
Winnipeg, MB R3J 0N6
(204) 831-1999

For Further Reading

Bender, David, and Bruno Leone. *Drug Abuse*. San Diego, CA: Greenhaven Press, Inc., 1994.

Hutchings, Donald. *Methadone*. New York: Chelsea House Publishers, 1992.

O'Donnell, Bea Rawls, and Gwen Johnson. *Drugs and Where to Turn*. Rev. ed. New York: Rosen Publishing Group, 1993.

Schnoll, Sidney. *Getting Help*. New York: Chelsea House Publishers, 1992.

Silverstein, Alvin, Virginia Silverstein, and Robert Silverstein. *The Addiction's Handbook*. Hillside, NJ: Enslow Publishers, Inc., 1991.

Smith, Sandra Lee. *Heroin*. New York: Rosen Publishing Group, 1995.

State Methadone Treatment Guidelines. U.S. Department of Health and Human Services, Substance Abuse and Mental Health Service Administration Center for Substance Abuse Treatment. Rockville, MD, 1993.

Woods, Geraldine. *Heroin*. Hillside, NJ: Enslow Publishers, Inc., 1994.

Index

About the Author

Carolyn Simpson teaches psychology at Tulsa Community College in Tulsa, Oklahoma. She has worked as a clinical social worker at mental health facilities in both Maine and Oklahoma, and is currently an outpatient therapist at Family Mental Health Center, a division of Parkside, Inc., in Tulsa.

Photo Credits

pp. 2, 48 by Ira Fox; p. 36 by Lauren Piperno; p. 19 © Archive Photos/Bob Scott; cover and all other photos by John Novajosky